eating disorder:

something deeper

BOBBIE GORE

ISBN: 1481168177
ISBN-13: 9781481168175

To people with eating disorder, their loved ones, and all who are dedicated to their recovery.

contents

It is by logic that we prove, but by intuition that we discover.
— Henri Poincare

How wonderful we have been met with a paradox. Now we have some hope of making progress.
— Neils Bohr

INTRODUCTION

In this book, you will find a new concept of eating disorder. For the most part, it is carefully formulated to replace pain and confusion with hope and understanding. This book began in a flash of intuition, however, this insight was only the surface. Seemingly unrelated bits of information needed to be pieced together at deeper levels. Although the work proved overwhelming, there was no turning back.

With the reader in mind, the goal is for the whole picture to emerge quickly and to provide practical and spiritual tools for recovery. Using an accelerated approach requires an openness to unfamiliar terms and unproven ideas. As stated, intuition began this book, and now, your intuition, as to whether the concepts resonate as true and useful, completes it. At the very least, you will experience a perspective of eating disorder that is unique and comforting.

Anorexia and bulimia, viewed as a continuum, offers a profound message for humanity. Of course, there are more transparent and positive ways of expressing this message. Looking through this disease long enough to perceive valuable testament is naturally difficult, but in doing so, the suffering of the anorexic and bulimic is exceedingly less meaningless.

PART ONE:

Healing the
Nourishment
Process

Order is what exists before you start arranging things.
— Marty Rubin

For nothing matters except life; and, of course order.
— Virginia Woolf

CHAPTER 1

• •

restore

This chapter is a straight forward approach to restore order to disordered eating. Let's begin with the first dimension of the nourishment process. Hunger, eat, digest, and metabolize is a simple description. But the best description is: sensory, consumption, digestion, and metabolism. Furthermore, these four nourishment mechanisms are cyclic, or open and close in specific order. We need a quick overview of their function to utilize the recovery steps.

HUNGER

To nourish, the sensory mechanism begins the cycle. Of course, food aroma, sight, and sound stimulate hunger pangs and digestive secretions. This nourishment mechanism also works through the thoughts and emotions. For example, we imagine the flavor and texture of traditional meals or food that comforts. We also use logic or step-by-step planning to obtain or prepare food.

EAT

Next, the consumption mechanism opens. Sensual pleasure in the aromas, flavors, and textures during food consumption is the best example of how the nourishment mechanisms work together. Here is something important to remember: eating can be thought of as the pinnacle nourishment mechanism.

DIGEST

Next, the digestion mechanism opens completely. (At this stage, the consumption mechanism has closed, however, the sensory mechanism remains open a bit longer sensing stomach fullness and digestion.) Digestive secretions and peristaltic movement empties the stomach.

METABOLIZE

The final mechanism in the cycle is metabolism: nutrients and vital substances or *information* builds, repairs, and provides energy. Metabolism can be described as continuous and also as extending around into the sensory mechanism.

The following steps protect and support the orderly cycle of the nourishment mechanisms from destructive impulses and behaviors:

1. Admit there is no healing, wholeness, or freedom without the nourishment mechanisms cycling forward.

2. Trust the orderly design or intelligence of the nourishment mechanisms above any impulse to control food, eating, and weight.

3. Respect food as information for the mental, emotional, and physical being.

4. Allow intuitive craving for foods that will correct nutritional deficiencies.

5. Admit that restricting pressure-loads impulses that recoil into bingeing.

6. Admit that purging or emptying the stomach causes more bingeing episodes.

7. Do not disorder the metabolism through laxatives, diuretics, drugs, or excessive exercise.

8. Admit that it is more destructive to break the orderly cycle of the nourishment mechanisms than breaking eating rules or food lists.

9. Do not use the failure to consume pure or low calorie food as reasoning or as permission to further binge or purge.

10. Do not think of food as an impure, harmful substance that must be restricted or purged.

11. Follow the order of the mechanisms through the fear or confusion of what, when, why and how to eat.

12. Admit that the quantity or amount of food consumed is more important than the quality or type of food consumed.

We are the country that has more food to eat than any in the world, and more diets to keep us from eating it.
— anonymous

The community must create the environment that maximizes the potential for people to make healthy choices.
— Chris Reynolds

CHAPTER 2

· ·

excess

The nourishment environment is the second dimension of the nourishment process. This expansive dimension influences what, when, why, and how we eat. A *nutrient-dense nourishment environment* has everything to do with the ability to nourish ourselves and remain healthy; whereas, a *disordered nourishment environment of empty foodstuff* is the trojan horse of most illness.

Although symptoms, diagnosis, and treatments vary, in fact, the disordered nourishment environment is an underlying cause of not only eating disorder, but also degenerative and metabolic disease. The increasing number of children with obesity, diabetes, and heart disease is the truest measure or illustration of this tragedy. Is it acceptable that the nourishment environment, the appetite, and the metabolism of children be overtaken with high fat, sugar, and salt foodstuff? Of course, you find this is unacceptable and affirm corrective action. But what is the best overall prevention for this health crisis or epidemic?

For effective disease prevention to manifest, a nourishment environment that is ordered with nutrient-dense food must be created. In other words, nourishment environments that are disordered need transforming. Consumers must lead this transformation by implementing new ways of eating. Unfortunately, consumers are addicted to fatty, sugary, and salty foodstuff.

Of course, we cannot ignore the fact that commercially driven mass-marketed and distributed foodstuff is easy to abuse. Consumers must resist subliminal marketing and the overwhelming amounts of unhealthy and available foodstuff that is habitually craved or that promises a new taste sensation. Clearly, nourishment environments disorder when poor eating habits combine with profit-driven food corporations.

Truth be told, our modern nourishment environment provides sustenance and convenience, but this pre-cooked, pre-packaged lifestyle is exacting various forms of pay-back. One form of pay-back is that mass-marketed and distributed high fat, sugar, and salt products cannot balance the nourish-ment mechanisms. To be specific, this addictive, high-calorie, low-nutrient foodstuff disorders both appetite and metabo-lism. This is significant when trying to understand bulimia and anorexia.

Let's begin with two simple equations or connections. Now, it is very simple to follow the connection between a disor-dered nourishment environment of *excess foodstuff* and that of *excess eating* and *weight.*

And the second equation is also simple to follow, the con-nection between a disordered nourishment environment of *food scarcity* and that of *malnourishment* and *starvation.* Painfully, the first and second equations follow cause and effect.

But, the third equation that we are seeking does not seem to follow cause and effect. I am speaking of *anorexia, or self-induced starvation occurring in an environment glutted with excess foodstuff.* For our present needs, we must find the connection or that which also follows cause and effect in anorexia. Let's look closer.

Needless to say, most people approve and consider it a personal success when restricting foodstuff for reasons along the lines of healing, spirituality, and self-improvement. I am sure you agree, this reasoning is popular and good-intentioned. However, as in the case of anorexia, good intention turns into a tragic failure because restricted foodstuff is not replaced with the proper amount of nourishment. The anorexic goes too far controlling the diet. A dangerous line is crossed. And of no less concern, the bulimic also crosses a dangerous line by bingeing and purging.

It can be said that, anorexia is the inability to eat and bulimia is the inability to stop eating. Although such behaviors or compulsions are opposite, the anorexic and bulimic are equally obsessed with food. Why is this? The most obvious answer, because equally for both, food is the necessary agent or means of control. Certainly, plentiful calories or excess foodstuff allows the disease of bulimia to exist. And yet, one can see that available calories or food allows the disease of anorexia to persist.

Yes, it is difficult to understand the unyielding response, the persistent self-starvation in a disordered nourishment environment having abundant, plentiful foodstuff. But it is not difficult to understand that an environment of excess foodstuff can drive the sensory mechanism toward obsession and the consumption mechanism toward compulsion. In some individuals this kind of environment causes an abnormal relationship or behavior with food, eating, and weight *(bingeing, purging, dieting,* and *restricting).* In other words, it is easy to lose the ability to nourish oneself in a disordered nourishment environment of fast, cheap, and empty foodstuff. Eventually, this inability or instability shows itself in *more than one form.*

Consider this important and telling fact: it is not uncommon, nor is it mere coincidence that anorexics often become bulimic. As one may well suspect, restricting or self-starvation in the midst of an addictive food environment is an overwhelming battle. The anorexic reaches a tipping point and "falls" into bulimia, of course, it is not desirable that one extreme is exchanged for the other. However, bulimia has a greater window or residual of life-saving calories than anorexia.

In addition, the transmutation of anorexia into bulimia strongly suggests a single solution or preventative. This is significant, because in seeking out a single solution to prevent both anorexia and bulimia should we not consider the *expansive nourishment environment as a safety net?* In other words, our first concern is a nourishment environment that contains the proper nutrition, information, or stimuli to prevent consumption levels from falling into the extremes or into the opposites of starving and bingeing. Although not complete protection, why take a chance on anything but this? A balanced nourishment environment is the support needed to naturally balance eating and weight and more importantly, to prevent the obsession and compulsion for both dieting and overeating. Is this the connection we are seeking or the cause and effect hiding in plain sight?

The final equation seems simple and self-evident: until we are surrounded by a nourishment environment that is ordered with whole, nutrient-dense food there will be needless suffering from eating disorder. The argument for this is simple: the extremely sensitive nourishment mechanisms are easily overwhelmed in a disordered nourishment environment of addictive-type foodstuff.

Anyway you look at it, humanity must have whole nourishment environments to reach full potential. This means healthy brain function, and of course, healthy bodies. This is why our country's retired military generals want junk-food removed from schools. A much higher intention can be found in the famous chefs who combine a knowledge of whole, fresh, quality food with culinary skill to provide much needed education, activism, and healing. We will come back to the subject of intention or purpose.)

To sum up, eating disorder is a symptom of a disordered nourishment environment. It is important that consumers vote with their dollars and exert positive pressure on the food companies. In other words, as individuals, families, and communities are able to eat healthier, so too, a healthier nourishment environment develops, This will prevent not only eating disorder, but many other diseases.

As for now, the nourishment mechanisms can be reset or restored with added support.

The free will is never free it is always attached to an object,
a purpose.
— Joyce Cary

There are no edges to my loving now.
— Rumi

~e~

CHAPTER 3

• •

direction

The third, and final dimension of the nourishment process is best described as the *purpose of compassion*. Simply stated, someone or something is leading the nourishment mechanisms, especially the consumption mechanism. We need to know, who or what is leading, and above all, is the direction unhealthy or healthy?

A variety of purposes give direction to food and eating. One person may take-up gourmet cooking to meet new people. Another person may consume hot-dogs as a competitive sport. I am sure you can easily identify a couple more purposes. What about weight loss? Undoubtedly, this must come to mind.

Let me say a few words about the purpose of weight loss: it lacks genuine intelligence and dependability to order the nourishment mechanisms. In fact, this purpose alone, brings temporary results to those who diet, but this is fortunate, compared to the damaging results it brings to those with chronic eating disorder. The important point being, *purpose* is the interface between *order* and *disorder* of the nourishment mechanisms.

The good news is the consumption mechanism can be bonded to a higher purpose and thus, automatically restore order to the nourishment mechanisms. To be specific, the higher the purpose, the higher the order. What does this mean? Although eating is a physical act, there is a higher purpose: eating as a spiritual act of nourishment. That is to say, nourishment contains vitamins, minerals, and other elements as information. This information signals or creates the gift of mental, emotional, and physical wholeness.

This is not saying, that you are choosing to disorder the nourishment mechanisms, and furthermore, this having happened to you is not surprising. Why? Because many people unwisely rid weight and many people unwisely eat to excess. The truth is, you have no intention of choosing eating disorder over the gift of wholeness. But unlike most people, you feel entirely controlled by something outside yourself. This feeling is understandable. In fact, there are deeper, hidden forces disordering the nourishment process.

But more to the point, what do we absolutely know about anorexia and bulimia? We know that the purpose of weight control through starving and purging is destructive. Also, that existence becomes a grotesque fusion of *food, eating, addiction, abuse,* and *isolation*. Again, why would you, or anyone choose this? Of course, this proves that no one really chooses anorexia or bulimia as an easy way to escape or control painful thoughts and emotions. No matter how or why eating disorder begins, choosing a higher purpose for food and eating brings it to an end.

So, we need to identify a higher purpose for food and eating that is true and present, and if this purpose is exactly opposite to weight control and isolation, all the better. Right? Let me assure you, this does exist in the *purpose of nourishment and connectedness to a whole self, others, and reality.*

Now, we have identified two purposes that lead in opposite directions. There should be little difficulty in recognizing the unhealthy purpose from the healthy one. Or, have I failed to make this clear? If not, (taking a hard line approach) your immediate responsibility is to let go of the unhealthy, destructive purpose. This is the difficulty now facing you. Why so difficult? Because you have a dependence on controlling food, eating, and weight. It's not easy, when you want to be free of eating disorder and yet, feel equally trapped by it. Perhaps, recovery may seem too complicated. For now, all you must do is ask, will I choose nourishment and connectedness or weight control and isolation? Ask, will I eat to nourish and accept weight gain or starve and purge? Meeting the truth inside yourself and eating disorder is where hope and healing begins, so let us consider the best evidence.

It is evident that until you turn away from starving and purging, loved ones must interface with the destruction and horror of eating disorder. Indeed, those who love you hold a vision of wholeness for you and the hope for your complete healing. True direction is the responsibility for your individual being or how your purpose for food and eating affects others, and the strength to follow true direction, is the heartfelt desire to be whole for loved ones.

In this breath, why not embrace the feeling of nourishment and connectedness to a whole self, others, and reality? All at once, why not embrace food and eating; care of the mental, emotional, and physical being; and family together as one? Ultimately, you will find that you have embraced the purpose and the direction of compassion, where eating becomes an act of truth and creation, instead of a pawn of false and destructive forces.

Now, you have an idea of the three dimensions of the nourishment process: the nourishment mechanisms, nourishment environment, and the purpose of compassion. It is important to know and revisit that, compassion fulfills the highest order of the nourishment process. Eating is more than a biological function of chewing, swallowing, and filling stomach space.

Although eating is a physical act of consuming or taking in, the approach must be a spiritual act of giving. Consumption, the pinnacle or *highest nourishment mechanism,* must be bonded to the highest purpose, compassion.

Some of us think holding on makes us strong
but sometimes it is letting go.
— Herman Hesse

If you had a different concept of yourself,
everything would be different.
— Neville

CHAPTER 4

• •

vision

This chapter looks at identity, eating disorder, and recovery in a radically different or imaginative way.

Eating disorder is a **false self:**

◆ that seeks to change, control, or perfect.

◆ *that causes pain and suffering only seeing incomplete and imperfect parts of existence.*

◆ that breaks existence down through blaming, shaming, and hiding.

◆ *that regrets the past, fears the future, and rejects the present moment.*

◆ that judges and labels the mental, emotional, and physical being as not enough or as unworthy.

The false self or the illusion of food, eating, and weight control leads to obsession, compulsion, addiction, and abuse. But after a time, the mental, emotional, and physical having suffered long, or having much destroyed, will no longer follow. At last, the search inside the void of eating disorder ends.

The steepest, most direct path away from eating disorder is to let go of a separate identity that is compared to others and judged as less. You must also let go of blaming self, others, conditions, and circumstances. Most of all, let go of the thoughts and the emotions rejecting the outer existence or the physical and material. This letting go, or this non-judgement is a place of being that allows the mental, emotional, and physical to ultimately receive food as nourishment.

Spiritual Vision does not condemn the **mental, emotional,** and **physical:**

◆ to eating less and weighing less.

◆ *to abusing food to get through painful experiences.*

◆ to dependence upon that which cannot be controlled.

◆ *to worth dependent on food, eating, weight, or the physical image.*

Eating disorder is a spiritual hunger or starvation, that must be fed by observing self, others, and existence from the stillness of non-judgement. This way of observing balances the thoughts and emotions. Ultimately, the behaviors toward food, eating, and weight are balanced. In other words, the oneness or wholeness of non-judgement balances the extreme, conflicted, painful parts of the false self and this prevents acting-out or disordering of the nourishment mechanisms.

Who you believe yourself to be, is how you will ultimately care for all. Do you believe that you are imperfect and therefore, unworthy? Do you believe that your existence is not as meaningful as others? If `yes´ comes to mind — this is the false self answering. It is clear, the false self is too limited and fragmented to nourish the mental, emotional, and physical being. Put it this way, the false self, or anorexia and bulimia sees extremes or opposites and this disorders the nourishment mechanisms. There is another way of seeing.

Spiritual Vision does not condemn the **thoughts** and **emotions**:

◆ to good and bad.

◆ *to fat and thin.*

◆ to beautiful and ugly.

◆ *to perfection and failure.*

Spiritual Vision does not condemn the **behaviors**:

◆ to food abuse and weight control.

◆ *to binge and purge.*

◆ to hunger and the denial to eat.

◆ *to self-starvation and the denial of nourishment.*

◆ to parts of self shown outwardly and abused parts of self hidden from others.

The best hope for removing self-abuse or self-hatred is to question who you believe, or imagine yourself to be. What do you believe about yourself? Who are you? Before answering, get a safe distance from the body, feelings, and thoughts. Do not rely on human senses or experiences. Why? Because of the judging, labeling, dividing, or separating parts self and existence. This is too emotional, too painful. We must unplug from an identity that is incomplete or imperfect. Better to observe human identity from a place of being that is above, greater, or higher. Better to observe human drama as a matrix-like illusion, an illusion that does not affect the real you.

Although the illusion seems painful and appears destructive at times, it is nonetheless worthy of loving observation. At some point, all that exists has a perfect need to be observed with compassion. This is the spiritual vision that heals or saves. So, the crux of the problem is that spiritual blindness can cause bodily starvation. Right? This spiritual vision or spiritual nourishment of compassion must be fulfilled, to receive food as secondary nourishment. Imagine, you are the spiritual vision of love that observes with oneness, connectedness, forgiveness, and compassion.

Inspiration is found in comic book and movie superheroes that are perfect or more powerful than human. Not only in fantasy, inspiration is also found in truth. Truth is, you are more than a limited human being. In fact, you are the opposite of human limitation, and ultimately this works perfectly. Perfection is the realization that your true being is present to care, present to heal, and present to give strength to the mental, emotional, and physical being. Imagine the human part turning toward your true being, receiving worth and strength to care for all.

True being continually expands from this center: love moving outward, encompassing others. Indeed, desire to give, or gratitude for that which is received is the best defense and the quickest way to remove confusion, fear, self-pity, or despair. Your true being is the perfect countermeasure to the thoughts and emotions that painfully contract, and to the self-identity that is small and meaningless. Spiritual vision of true being is too connected and expansive to be insignificant, abandoned, and unloved. Imagine your highest worth and your highest purpose is the love that is your true being.

Belief in higher worth and higher purpose gives strength to care for self and others. In other words, the ability to believe and the ability to care is not separate. Healing occurs when something new and trustworthy takes the place of eating disorder. Especially, something beyond superficial appearances and reflections; beyond self, others, circumstances, and conditions. Yes, beyond failure, judgement, isolation, control, and power!

For the believer, spiritual vision is without the failed, hated parts of self and existence. To observe with compassion, forgiveness, and acceptance is most of the wholeness needed to balance the thoughts, emotions, and behaviors. In other words, this prevents the painful or fragmented parts of being that turn against each other as abuse.

Spiritual Vision of True Being as the Space and Grace of Love is to observe failure, judgement, isolation, control, and power as false separation from the Holy and Sacred Place of Oneness that balances all in Forgiveness and Gratitude.

If this spiritual place of being, way of observing, worth, and purpose is not something you are ready to trust, no matter. Instead, trust the orderly cycle of the nourishment mechanisms. Clearly, this order or design is the most down-to-earth support that exists. My personal story is one of recovery from bulimia through Christianity and the desire for wholeness. Facing painful experiences with the belief in true being lifts the thoughts and emotions to a place of comfort. This comfort restores sanity and freedom. With that said, all that remains is to seek, ask, pray for the guidance and strength that is from above, from God.

You suppose you are the trouble
But you are the cure
You suppose that you are the lock on the door
But you are the key that opens it
It's too bad that you want to be someone else
You don't see your own face, your own beauty
Yet, no face is more beautiful than yours.

— Rumi

Part Two:
Eating Disorder
Exposed

First appearance deceives many.
— Ovid

If you care to look beneath the surface of appearances, you will most likely find an "aha" or two.
— Oprah Winfrey

CHAPTER 5

. . . .

surface

That many people diet, without descending into eating disorder obscures a negative force beneath. When in fact, beneath
the surface of dieting there is a *power-prejudice*, that is to say,
one side increases social and material power and the other
side diminishes this. It is clear, power is given to individuals
who meet the cultural ideal of thinness and is denied to those
who do not. It is like two-sides of the same coin and although
one side appears positive, it is a false positive.

It is likely, the power-prejudice can extend through a mindset that is slanted toward extremes. To explain further, all or nothing, black and white thinking are tendencies that go-along with the two-sided power of weight loss and prejudice of weight gain.

The obvious problem is that dieting becomes a false measure disconnected from health and wholeness; impulses and behaviors to control mere ounces and inches becomes the over-arching distortion or dictate.

However, to understand the severe or lethal behaviors of eating disorder it is important to look deeper. One must look through the *dieting,* through the *power-prejudice,* into the depths of *over-sexualization.* Let me explain, as sexual images expand through mass-media, the power-prejudice of weight also expands into the nourishment mechanisms of men, women, and children. Again, as social and material power intertwines with sexuality, so too, a kind of chasm or void opens. And in this void, fatal impulses and behaviors to control weight arise.

Tragically, there are various forms of social, capital, and political forces disordering the nourishment process. In fact, the anorexic is often compared to a victim of a concentration camp. We must ask ourselves, is this comparison revealing more than we realize. In other words, is there a hidden common denominator?

Of course, anorexia is self-induced starvation and therefore, is not equal to forced systematic-starvation, as compared, this appears to be a true statement of the facts. On the other hand, we can compare a political hunger-strike (a form of self-induced starvation used to protest oppression) to anorexia. And, the two-forms of self-induced starvation are not equal to each other. But this is not the relevant point of focus.

Let's compare the political hunger-strike, or the use of self-induced starvation to protest, control, and overthrow tyrannical oppression with the reverse use of systematic-starvation by a tyrant or dictatorship to control and oppress others. Does this final comparison or strange reversal not strike you? Do you see, whether victim or victimizer, whether the oppressed or the oppressor, the nourishment process becomes a vulnerable or misused target, taking a similar, ruinous hit of malnourishment and starvation?

For the sake of better understanding, all of this needs to be brought together. One way to do this, is to say, that on a scale of control and oppression, the political hunger-strike is registering somewhere between the systematic-starvation in a concentration camp and the anorexic. Rather than saying that the three-forms of malnourishment and starvation are wholly equal, this is saying that the striking similarities indicate a similar or equally destructive force present. Specifically, a degree of *control* and *oppression* has surfaced in, or has targeted the nourishment process of the *prisoner,* the *protester,* and the *anorexic.* Have we found the common denominator in all three-forms? If you agree that anorexia is about control or that over-sexualization is ultimately oppressive, then indeed, we have. Without a doubt, it is not unusual for control and oppression to disorder the nourishment process.

And of no less importance, is the question of how this relates to bulimia. To find out, the next chapter brings us back to the dual forces shaping and expanding the destructive impulses and behaviors in anorexia and bulimia. I am referring to the power-prejudice and the disordered nourishment environment of harmful foodstuff.

Just as we have two eyes and two feet, duality is part of life.
— Carlos Santana

Our mind is capable of passing beyond the dividing line we have drawn for it. Beyond the pairs of opposites of which the world consists other new insights begin.
— Herman Hesse

CHAPTER 6

●

construct

As explained earlier, although dieting and weight loss seem positive, the overall force of the power-prejudice is too negative. The power-prejudice takes over generating fear and despair around food, eating, and weight. Unchecked, this builds or concentrates into phobia, obsession, and compulsion. And this concentrated, negative force controls the individual to restrict or disorder the nourishment mechanisms.

Recall that there is a second force that is also exerting control on the anorexic and bulimic, as you have probably guessed, the disordered nourishment environment of excess foodstuff. Existence can become unbalanced due to the extremes of the power-prejudice pulling toward dieting or weight loss, while at the same time, the disordered nourishment environment is pulling toward excess eating and weight. Anorexia and bulimia is the individual's misguided attempt to exist upon this unnatural construct or continuum of opposing forces — an existence of serious self-destruction or violence. And yet, behaviors surfacing as *dieting, starving, purging, and bingeing* are superficially dismissed as being illogical or ridiculous.

A more reasonable, and therefore more respectful understanding can begin with the idea that anorexia and bulimia is a single disease and as such, the symptoms can be logically explained. Let's take a closer look. To fully understand, you must view eating disorder as a continuum. The first point (starve) and the second point (purge) share one end of the continuum, and the third point (binge) is at the opposite end.

Or, one can take the basic view of a line representing food, eating, and weight. Don't forget, one end represents restriction and the opposite end represents excess. But, this view is too basic and more importantly, does not serve us well. Why? Because, if we fail to see eating disorder as a continuum that is partly complementary and partly opposed, we may fail to understand that anorexia and bulimia is a single disease having impulses and behaviors that are partly alike, and partly opposite. The anorexic restricts food, the bulimic abuses food, but both restrict weight. A side-by-side comparison of the dominant

44

tendencies, or the first, second, and third points of the continuum may be the best way to prevent misunderstanding. Perhaps
then, we can move forward with the knowledge that radically
different behaviors that appear totally separate are, in fact, inti-
mately related.

The anorexic is held at the adjacent points of starve and
purge. Of course, the anorexic tendency, or the impulses and
behaviors are a narrow shift between starving and purging.
Accordingly, movement at this end of the continuum is focused
or constricted. As a result, there can be a temporary sense of
control, security, and accomplishment.

The bulimic is held at the opposite points of purge and
binge. Of course, the bulimic tendency, or the impulses and
behaviors are a wide shift between purging and bingeing.
Accordingly, movement between opposing points of the continuum is radical or chaotic. As a result, there can be a temporary
sense of losing control, insecurity, and failure in the bulimic,
particularly after bingeing.

Before going any further, can agree on the following per-
spectives? Such as, dieting and overeating are unhealthy
because this is the surface of eating disorder and in some
cases, the initiation into anorexia and bulimia. Also, it is
misleading to use the term: binge-purge cycle. As stated, a
healthy relationship with food and eating has a predictable
rhythm or an orderly cycle. When talking about the disease
of anorexia and bulimia, we are talking about something very
different: polarization and movement between extremes. You
see, the anorexic tendency is to fixate to one extreme, while

45

the bulimic tendency is an abrupt shift between extremes. Of course, the movement, the positioning, or the degree of disordering along the continuum should be considered on an individual basis.

I hope you have a basic understanding of eating disorder as a continuum. To clarify, starving and bingeing are the outermost points and purging is the shared point. (Both the anorexic and the bulimic purge to control weight.) In addition, the power-prejudice supports the starving and purging end of the continuum and the disordered nourishment environment of excess foodstuff supports the bingeing end. In the next chapter we will discover that the purpose of compassion meets this duality, or this unnatural tension of opposites head-on.

To understand is to perceive patterns.
— Isaiah Berlin

Order is never observed; it is disorder that attracts attention because it is awkward and intrusive.
— Eliphas Levi

CHAPTER 7

●●●●●●●●●●●●●●●●●●●●●●●●●●●

proof

It is an important observation that dieting is the opposite of overeating, and likewise, that starving is the opposite of binge-ing. Now, this pattern of opposites is a clue. Let me explain, for any destructive force present in eating disorder there is likely an opposite force. Recall that the power-prejudice and the dis-ordered nourishment environment of excess are opposed. Also recall that the two opposed forces rise up as a continuum of disordered eating, or as extreme impulses and behaviors.

As mentioned earlier, to understand eating disorder, especially anorexia and bulimia, you must look deeper. If you are willing to do so, you will see that anorexia and bulimia bubble up from over-sexualization and over-commercialization of food, eating, and weight. At the same time, you will see that over-sexualization is a form of oppression and that over-commercialization is a form of greed. (I use the term greed to simply describe: foodstuff pushed for profit without regard for human health.) Here is the problem, the nourishment process of the anorexic and bulimic is dominated by these forces.

But more importantly, is realizing what should be dominating the nourishment process. What should take the place of forces that are opposed to one another and to the nourishment process? What should take the place of deep underlying forces like oppression and greed? The only answer is all encompassing care of self, family, humanity, and creation.

In our relationship to food and eating the spiritual is always the most practical. Let me explain, the nourishment process is not an open system, it is self-organizing. Recall, that this system consists of the nourishment mechanisms, the nourishment environment, and the purpose of compassion. Think of the purpose of compassion as a kind of invisible force-field. This being said, the definite effects of this field, meaning as to whether it is present or non-present, can be rightly seen. When present, this field organizes or unifies social, capital, and political forces to protect and support the nourishment process. Without this field, there is a certainty of disordered nourishment mechanisms and nourishment environments. In fact, the nourishment process is a biological indicator of this invisible field of compassion. If there is any disordering of the nourishment process, first, suspect a void of compassion.

Starvation is a clear indication that the field is displaced. For example, social, capital, and political power fuse with the nourishment process. Sex, money, politics, malnutrition, hunger-strikes, and systematic starvation form into grotesque schisms that displace the purpose or field of compassion. In other words, the simple and innocent hunger for food tragically combines with the manipulative and guilty hunger for power. Some evidence of this exists throughout history.

In most cases, certain forces seeking power and having a void of compassion are often difficult to identify and contain because they are far-reaching or surface slowly over time. But sooner or later, any significant void of compassion will leave its mark of disease and suffering in the nourishment process. And, its mark shall be understood or, as in the case of anorexia and bulimia, labeled an enigma. However, from this perplexing disorder or disease, it is possible to gain the knowledge of compassion and thus, protect the nourishment process from all forms of destabilization and disordering.

Now, one may incorrectly assume that eating disorder is not significantly different from other physical addictions or substance abuse. Of course, the differences can be explained. First of all, social and capital forces are allowed to perpetuate anorexia and bulimia. Second, the disease is centered or arises out of a biological process. And finally, the third and profound difference from other addiction, abuse, and mental illness is a pattern of opposites.

The phenomena surrounding anorexia and bulimia pretty much line-up horizontally and vertically. Down one column: dieting, anorexia, the power-prejudice of weight or over-sexualization finally leads to oppression. Down the opposing column: overeating, bulimia, the fast, cheap, addictive foodstuff or over-commercialization finally leads to greed. But these disturbances in the field of compassion, are not really final.

Amazingly, the clues or the straight lines that lead to oppression and greed having displaced compassion, also lead to the design of the nourishment process. What's more, this design is the mysterious work of an unrecognized source — *that is until the void of compassion left a peculiar, severe mark in the nourishment mechanisms of the anorexic and bulimic.* And given this, it is not only possible, but probable that when viewed together, anorexia and bulimia provide a message or perhaps something greater, a kind of proof. We find proof that the nourishment mechanisms are polarized by certain kinds of forces. Also, we find that a unifying field of compassion prevents this. The final proof that is offered through anorexia and bulimia is the preeminent or preordained compassionate design of the nourishment process.

On the other hand, using this evidence alone requires a tremendous leap of imagination, such a leap could be everything, or it could be nothing. However, if the highest order of the nourishment process is fulfilled in compassion, the solution is straight and narrow: lower purposes for food, sex, money, and power must be sacrificed. You may well ask, how will such

52

sacrifice ever take hold? The answer is found in humanity looking toward a greater need, and a greater work.

The nourishment process is connected to the medical, financial, and energy systems. No doubt, humanity needs an approach to quickly balance and unify these systems. And on top of this, there is a profound connection between individual freedom and the ability to nourish ourselves. What does this mean? Divisions that are set against each other or that seek to control, must be replaced by care that encompasses all.

Compassion may be the only single source or evolutionary path open that balances the collective need to survive and the individual desire to thrive. What choice exists beyond this? None that I can speak of. There is only the evolutionary work of unifying the spiritual and the material. True to benevolent design, there is only the compassion of oneness, as the highest purpose and the highest order of the nourishment process.

If we agree that our purposes evolve, we must also agree that there is no shortage of hopeful questioning. Starting with, is our most physical being, the nourishment process, an indicator for our most spiritual being, compassion? Or, is there enough evidence proving compassion is the highest purpose and the highest order of the nourishment process? And, if we accept any lesser design, are we not resigning ourselves to a universe that is without consciousness and therefore, impossible to trust or believe in? Is this our only hope, to proceed as if compassionate design is, was, and will be?

A human being is part of a whole, called by us universe,
a part limited in time and space. He experiences himself,
his thoughts and feelings as something separated from
the rest ... a kind of optical delusion of his consciousness.
This delusion is a kind of prison for us, restricting us to our
personal desires and affection for a few persons nearest
to us. Our task must be to free ourselves from this prison
by widening our circle of compassion to embrace all living
creatures and the whole of nature in its beauty.
— Albert Einstein

Made in the USA
San Bernardino, CA
16 October 2018